You know from science classes that pets need special care. They need food, water, and shelter. Suppose you had a dog. Where would it stay while you were at school? Could it stay in your home? Would a doghouse be a better choice?

Many people have doghouses for
their pets. Doghouses keep pets dry
when it rains or warm when it is cold.

Some places sell doghouses that have already been built. But, you might want to build your own doghouse.

Of course, it is faster to buy a doghouse. Building one will take many hours. Do what your heart and your wallet tell you to do.

You can find pictures of doghouses in books. You can also find plans for how to build them. Of course, the doghouse must be the right size for your dog.

If you do build a doghouse, be safe!
Always have an adult do the sawing.
Don't use tools without an adult helping
or watching.

Now, go change into work clothes.
You are ready to start your building
adventure!

Look at your plans carefully. Check
for any special tools you need. Put
everything together in one place. Follow
the plans step by step.

Measure each plank two times before having it cut. (That way you'll be sure to get the right length.) Build the floor, roof, and walls. Check your work at each step. Then put together the parts you built.

Sand the doorway so it is smooth to the touch. This will keep your dog's fur from getting caught. Put some straw on the doghouse floor. That will keep your dog warm and smelling sweet.

Now call your dog into its new home. Your special pet is sure to be happy there.